Interior Graphics/Art Credit:
Matt Allen Photography
Jeremy Ryan
Alisia K Photography

WestBow Press books may be ordered through booksellers or by contacting:

WestBow Press
A Division of Thomas Nelson & Zondervan
1663 Liberty Drive
Bloomington, IN 47403
www.westbowpress.com
1 (866) 928-1240

Because of the dynamic nature of the Internet, any web addresses or links contained in this book may have changed since publication and may no longer be valid. The views expressed in this work are solely those of the author and do not necessarily reflect the views of the publisher, and the publisher hereby disclaims any responsibility for them.

Any people depicted in stock imagery provided by Thinkstock are models, and such images are being used for illustrative purposes only. Certain stock imagery © Thinkstock.

ISBN: 978-1-9736-1367-1 (sc)
ISBN: 978-1-9736-1366-4 (e)

Library of Congress Control Number: 2017918746

Print information available on the last page.

WestBow Press rev. date: 1/22/2018

# Journey On

A PERSONAL COLLECTION OF THOUGHTS,
POEMS AND SHORT STORIES

## Lindsay Reith

# foreword

SOMETIMES IN THIS BUSY LIFE you need a little refreshment, an oasis for the weary soul. Sometimes we simply need purpose renewed. "Journey On" will surely give rest to the traveler, while rekindling the passion and burning drive that keeps each pilgrim moving forward. Lindsay takes you through personal moments in her journey and shares her heart in an honest and conversational style. You will be spiritually encouraged and urged to stop and smell the roses, spend time with family, friends and the people God has placed in your life. Truly an inspiration to dedicate every moment of your life to God, give Him the best and finish the race well.

We have known Lindsay personally for nearly 20 years and watched her grow from a little girl running around playing with our children, into a young woman, using what God has given her to reach the world. She has a gift for writing and sharing with the reader in a special way. Read it, live it and let the message of this book drive you forward with a renewed purpose as each of us...... "Journey On."

Michelle and Jim Bob Duggar
"19 Kids and Counting"

# *acknowledgments*

N<small>O ONE BECOMES WHO THEY</small> are or accomplishes what they do without individuals who have invested in them, believed in them, prayed for them and been there for them through it all. I would not be publishing this book today had it not been for people in my life who never gave up on me or believing that I could. "Could what?," you may ask. That I could be whatever God called me to be, accomplish whatever He asked me to do and if I was willing to sweat and toil I could achieve whatever dream God planted within my heart and go as far as I wanted to go. It is to these people I owe my life and it is to them I say, " thank you."

My Sweet Jesus, the Saviour of my soul- I love you and thank you for Redeeming this lost and wayward child. You have never given up on me, failed me or have not been there when I called out. You are the reason alone that I write this, my first published book, You are the topic, You are the One who can change any traveler's journey and make it one worth taking. As a little girl You gave me a passion to write, you instilled within me a love for it, poems and painting pictures with pretty words. You are the giver of good gifts and I thank you for giving me the opportunity to bring the humble gifts You gave me and lay them at Your feet. May You use this book for Your glory alone.

My Darling and amazing Mama and Daddy- You are God's hands on this earth, molding and making me into what He wanted, when I was too stubborn to understand. You have selflessly given your life and poured all you are and more into me, every day living with eternity in mind. I have been blessed beyond measure or what I deserve to experience such love and sacrifice. When I was very young, you recognized gifts that God had instilled within me. During my years as a little girl, writing tiny books, drawing and coloring the picture illustrations and then placing them in three ring binders and creating my own cover art. You believed in me and you encouraged me. You made me believe that it was possible to use these gifts for God and that one day it wouldn't be a three ring binder publication and crayon art on our bookshelf, but a work I could share with the world. Thank you for loving me unconditionally, always pointing me to Jesus and exhorting me to live my life for Him alone! Thank you for reading this book and helping me countless times with edits. I love you both more than words can say, well, I could try, but it would take several thousand volumes.

My dearest grandparents, Nonny and Pappy, MawMaw and Pawpaw- Where would I be without the love and support of my grandparents!? You have encouraged me and always believed I could, even when it looked kind of bleak at times. I have so many beautiful memories that have not only pulsated deep within me, but they have blossomed and helped make me who I am today. You are all in this book, you have inspired stories, you have inspired my life and I believe each of you will inspire every person who reads this book. Your influence is endless, your impact forever and your selfless, loving hearts beat within me and will begin to beat inside each person who picks up this book. I love you, I love you so much. Grandparents mean the world to their grandchildren and you have changed my world for the better, forever. Thank you so much.

My siblings, best friends and fellow life adventurers, Sarah, Emily and Matthew- Truly I see each of you as gifts straight from Heaven to my life. I cannot fathom walking this journey without each of you, together learning and growing. We have always been best friends, (I'm so glad Mom and Dad made sure of that!) and I love you more than cheesecake, kayaking or the color orange, and that's a lot!!! Each of you have helped me grow, always been honest with me and loved the real me on my worst days. You are always there for me and I can count on you, no matter what. Thank you for listening to me brainstorm this book. Sarah, thanks for helping your technologically challenged sister email files and other things that stump my mind! Emily, thank you for listening to me talk about ideas and listening to sections and giving awesome and honest feedback! Matt, thank you for taking nearly half of the beautiful photos inside this publication and producing the greatest promo video ever! Each of you have played a vital role and I would not be at this point without you. Thank you to my bestest friends!

Special thanks to Jim Bob and Michelle Duggar for graciously forwarding this book. Special thanks to Andy Andrews, Eric Bennett and Kevin Williams for so kindly endorsing and supporting this work!

I want to thank you, whoever you are holding this book in your hands at this moment. Thank you for supporting this, loving me and encouraging my life by the fact that you are reading the book right now! Thank you and I love you!

Grateful To Journey On With Each Of You,
Lindsay

Dear Traveler,

This life is a journey. Our ultimate destination is Heaven. The road in between holds many unknowns. What is my purpose, calling, direction or gifts? It is in these moments of searching that we must trust The Mapmaker. Knowing He has set us on this course and He will perfect every detail of our pilgrimage. This book is an oasis of encouragement for our travelers, the pilgrims. This is for you dear wayfaring stranger. May every mountain you climb and every bend you round bring you closer to the place God has prepared for you. Godspeed as you Journey On.

Lindsay

Hebrews 11:13- 16- "These all died in faith, not having received the promises, but having seen them afar off, and were persuaded of them, and embraced them, and confessed that they were strangers and pilgrims on the earth. For they that say such things declare plainly that they seek a country. And truly, if they had been mindful of that country from whence they came out, they might have had opportunity to have returned. But now they desire a better country, that is, an heavenly: wherefore God is not ashamed to be called their God: for he hath prepared for them a city."

Don't forsake your dreams. Embed them in your soul. Write them on the template of your mind. Carve them on the surface of your heart. Hold them in front of you at all times. Loosely enough that God can take them, but tightly enough the naysayers can't snatch them.

If someone or something starts to rain on the parade God has you in, pull out your umbrella and carry on.

# *journey on for the future*

DURING MY MID TO LATE teens we gifted my Daddy with a hive of honeybees for Father's Day. This present brought many wonderful moments of learning and memories! It wasn't long at all after we gave him the hive that they colony of bees split or as it is called, "swarmed." Through this process a second hive was born and our little honey bee farm grew from one to two hives. I remember suiting up in proper " bee attire," something that resembles an astronaut's space suit! We were sure to leave no cracks or crevices in our armor. Giving no opportunity for the perturbed honeybee to try and stop our advance. We would waddle out in our moon suits and giant gloves and help Daddy check the hives, feed them sugar water and pull out frames of comb dripping with thick, golden nectar. I especially recall my sister Sarah and Daddy learning the hard way to never check a hive at night time. You see, normally those little stinkers are aggressive and boisterous. They swarm about you loudly and make a brave advance when you finally leave, generally chasing you a long ways, even to the front door of the house! But, at night time they don't do any of those things, they just quietly crawl. Crawl all over you and your suit and you can't hear them or detect where they are. Sarah and Daddy had gone out late to check the bees and it was a creepy, crawly catastrophe! They had bees all over them that were subdued in the dark, but would surely sting at first opportunity. I remember Sarah freaking out as she began to take her suit off and bees were still on it and creeping through her hair! A night we shall never forget! One of the sweetest memories and I do mean sweetest, was our first honey harvest. What a day. We had long waited to collect that liquid gold from those combs, that were by now laden with their treasure. The day was full of friends, family and working together. Everyone joined the events. My grandparents, my uncle was in town and even friends visiting. There were the select who marched bravely to the hives like knights to battle in their shining armor. There was a team cutting the comb, spinning the comb and finally bottling it for the days ahead. One of the most vivid memories I have happened after the long day of hard work and dodging mad bees was over and done. It was peach season and Mama had several boxes of peaches that were just reaching that moment where you squeeze them and a little juice drips out. Always the ideal indication that they are supremely ripe to perfection. Mama also happened to make the world's richest and finest homemade ice cream that you have ever put inside your mouth. And here we were with jars of glistening, golden honey fresh from our farm sitting in our kitchen. You might say it all just lined up for one the most beautiful endings to a memorable day. Mama churned the homemade ice cream, we helped peel and cut the peaches and when it was all done, oh my! Homemade ice cream topped with syrupy fresh peaches and the diadem in the crown was honey, just moments fresh drizzled on top of it all! As soon as that honey hits

the freezing cold ice cream it just caramelized into thick strands of gold sparkling in my bowl. We sat around on our deck and in the kitchen and talked about the day, relishing the delicious product. As I look back now, I am struck by a truth that many of us will probably encounter at some point on our journey. Those little honeybees worked hard, everyday for the honey that filled their combs. It was a long process and took a lot of determination. They never stopped. Yet, there we were sitting on the deck eating and reaping the benefits of their hard labor. You know what's even more amazing? After that harvest, they

went right back to work again. It didn't stop them for a moment. Sometimes in life you are going to pour something into someone else, work hard to reach a heart or give all you've got to serve and you may never, ever, see the fruit of your efforts. You may never sit there and relish the results or bask in the bounty. You just might possibly be the one that sows, that gives, that serves and one day years from now the fruit of it will be harvested

in a life. It may be that you are striving for the generations to come that will surely reap the sweet harvest of your labor. But, never forget my friend, that God sees and God remembers. Just keep sowing, keep working, keep planting and rest knowing the harvest will come and lives will reap the sweet fruit for all eternity. Now that's a bounty to enjoy!

Pruning makes for prettier posies. Remember that when God heads your way with the pruning shears.

Don't ever forget that the dream you are living now is the one you dreamed yesterday. Remember this and be forever grateful when it comes true.

Smile at someone today. It may be the only one they receive -Wisdom From Nonny (My Dear Grandma)

Carry your own sunshine- Wisdom From Nonny

You will fail at some point my friend. Go ahead and accept that. The key to your success is deciding now that failure is never final and it only makes you more determined to succeed.

Be strategic, be deliberate, be thoughtful. Right now your choices are mapping out a road that your feet are going to walk for a long while. One day your life will unfold. That is the day you turn around and see the moments that brought you to where you are.

People say, "grow up." But, I find a certain quality in grown ups to be quite problematic. I believe there is a part of a child's heart that is to never leave us. The faith, trust, love and ability to dream and believe that anything can come true. Don't ever let that die, no matter how "grown up" you are.

When I was a small child I dreamed large, boundless dreams. Not every dream is meant to be or will come true. But, give them all to God. He will take the dreams He knows will be best for you and He will bring those to pass. Because one dream didn't come true might mean He has a better one waiting to unfold. But whatever you do, don't stop dreaming.

# journey on leaving a mark

ON OUR SMALL FARM IN Arkansas, I planted my first herb garden. Daddy helped me stake out a perfect square with nicely rounded edges. We tilled and fertilized the earth until it was soft and rich, ready for planting. I placed a small path leading diagonally through the garden with herbs and flowers billowing lushly on either side. This little piece of earth was such a delight to me! One of my prize plantings was an experimental crop of peanuts. The nuts themselves were given to us by a friend who grew them himself. So, Daddy helped me plant them and my nuts flourished wonderfully! The harvest finally came after growing healthily all season. They had produced a rich crop of perfectly shaped peanuts! I was ecstatic. What a unique and fun plant to grow and harvest. We washed the loose earth from off the nuts and arranged them on a rectangular baking pan. The plan was to roast them and then relish the flavor! We did roast them. Actually, that would be a gross understatement. You see, the pan with the peanuts was stored in our oven after the initial roasting and subsequently people would preheat the oven for another purpose and re- roast the nuts! No one would remember until the house was filled with the aroma of roasting peanuts! Those nuts went through so many countless roastings on that baking sheet that they eventually turned blackish in color and literally made dozens of peanut shaped imprints all over the pan! Permanently peanut stained, that pan was forever a humorous reminder of our rather failed attempt. The for sure thing was, they certainly left their mark, their imprint and the exact likeness of a peanut forever shadowed on the surface of that pan. What mark is your life leaving? Will anyone even see an imprint when you are gone or walk away? We should be so filled with Jesus that He is the impression, the imprint and mark that is indelibly left on people's hearts and minds. If the baking sheet was a room or a situation and you were the peanut, when you walked away, would others say, "we just saw Jesus here." Would you leave a shadow of godliness, love, hope and life in your absence. Believe me, it will last long after you walk out of the room or drive away. Let's take a lesson from that pan of peanuts today.

Sometimes you're perched on your comfortable branch in life and God says "jump, I'm down here to catch you." You just sit there thinking how secure it feels, how pretty the view is and how much you achieved getting up there. Then God comes up behind you, cuts the branch and says- "fly."

Always take time for children. Talk to them, love them, listen to them. Their voices are valuable, their stories important. They are our sunrises and sunsets of the future. This investment has eternal returns.

A sanctified imagination in a young person is one of the most powerful weapons they can wield for the Kingdom of God. A daring young heart who deems no mountain too high, no battle too hot, no foe too great and no task too difficult to accomplish for their Heavenly Captain. Their minds are fertile fields yielded to God, allowing whatever seed He plants to germinate, moreover grow and produce fruit that scares most to even consider. The majority of people are content to maintain mediocrity, but sanctified imaginations go where few walk and where God waits.

Instead of turning your nose up and casting a sideways glance at your brother or sister, why don't we come alongside, link arms and help them on their way. You might be surprised when you fall and they pick you up.

I have learned people will hurt you. But, it's much easier to let it go when I see me hammering the nails at Calvary and His wounded eyes meeting mine. You can easily forget what it was you were about to hold a grudge for.

May happiness bloom in your heart and soul and when it has blossomed there, may the world walk by and partake of its fragrance.

Bidding summer goodbye
With all its glory blooms
Knowing the breeze whispers still
A new season is coming soon
When the last rose drops her head
In quite, still repose
The trees ignite their fury full
In radiant reds and golds.
- Poem penned in 2016

# journey on when you are afraid

MONTHS AND MONTHS AND HOURS and hours of practice. The same song, the same notes infiltrated our home at an excessive and slightly annoying rate of repetition. At that age, about 15, I was kind of obsessed with this song. I mixed it with every possible melody that flowed and played it on the piano until my family was wishing they had ear plugs. The song was Canon in D. I was now infatuated with my latest arrangement for my upcoming Christmas recital. Canon In D and Silent Night. Oh, if you only new how well I knew this song. I mean, I could almost close my eyes and play it by memory. Practice was not lacking in this situation. Now, just as a side note here. I absolutely, completely and totally dreaded recitals. They were the pivotal events that happened generally twice a year, that if I could just survive through, the rest of my life would finally be ok. I was deathly afraid. I was terrified of being in front of crowds. I got shaky, my stomach hurt, it was actually in about a gazillion knots. I didn't see why we needed recitals. I mean, why can't I just play the song for my teacher and let her enjoy it??? Why did we have to torture ourselves twice a year?! In my mind it was pointless and painful, but as long as my parents and teachers had anything to do with it, I wasn't getting out of it. So at long last the night comes. We were supposed to play our pieces by memory if at all possible. Of course, I had mine by memory. I had only played it a thousand and one times it seemed. This shouldn't be a problem. Finally my name was next on that little program they print out at these events. I walk up on stage, sit down at the piano and begin the song that my family now almost knew by memory, just from the excess practice. My fingers touched the Ivory keys. I begin to press the Ivory keys. What happened next, to this day I cannot explain or rationalize. I couldn't for the life of me remember past the first few notes! My stomach was hurting and my mind was as blank as a black chalkboard. Nothing there! I'm thinking, who on earth forgets the piece they could play in their sleep?! Of course this only added to my pandemonium. So then it was a chain reaction, the more I freaked out, the more I forgot. Really not a lovely situation. By God's grace and believe me, He must have really known I needed help badly, I somehow muddled my way through the intro and made it through the song. I had never been so grateful to crawl off a platform in my life! Let me tell you friends, the fear was real. The same fear reared it's head when I was asked a few years later to lead an opening hymn at a women's meeting. I wanted to say, " no thank you." But, I knew that would be wrong. So, instead I just felt sick that evening and the next morning leading up to it. This was a struggle. I didn't want to be in front of people and please, oh please don't ask me to say anything to them!!! You know what I do every weekend of my life now? I stand in front of crowds of people, play and sing songs and......gasp...... talk to them!!! I think God must be smiling just a little bit. Seriously, I mean does this seem a little ironic and funny to anyone else? Here's the deal. God is not interested in what you feel comfortable with or think you are exceptionally great at. Matter of fact, the weaker you are, the more He can do. If there ever was a Moses looking at God saying, "I can't do this or say that!" It was me. It was like God said, "Here, watch this. Not what you can do Lindsay (because we all know what that was like). But, watch what I can do through you."

2 Corinthians 12:9 &10 –"And he said unto me, My grace is sufficient for thee: for my strength is made perfect in weakness. Most gladly therefore will I rather glory in my infirmities, that the power of Christ may rest upon me. Therefore I take pleasure in infirmities, in reproaches, in necessities, in persecutions, in distresses for Christ's sake: for when I am weak, then am I strong."

Friend, what is something in your life you have not given to God, because you feel inadequate and are afraid? Please hear me, from first hand experience. God is just waiting to show Himself mighty in your life. He is willing to take your insecurities and weaknesses and use them in powerful ways. The key is you must be willing to step outside your comfort zone and like Moses, surrender to His plan.

# journey on knowing the end result

HAVE YOU EVER THOUGHT ABOUT all the dumb things you did as a child and marvel that you have survived so long?! When I think back to some of our childhood escapades and daring adventures I shake my head in amazement that we made it! One particular day found me and my younger sister on the swing set that our Daddy built for us to enjoy and on which to let our playful imaginations run wild. We were passing the time swinging and suddenly we had the daring idea to twist our swing's chains, until they were tight and lifted us high, then we thought, we can bungee jump! Of course, bungee jump in a chain swing, seriously?! I don't know what we were thinking! I suppose we weren't. We proceeded with our plan and began twirling and twisting until the swings retracted so high in the air. We then stood upon the edge of the highest board we could find and gathered all our strength and bravery together. We counted off and jumped! It was about the shortest lived thing you could imagine. A very short fall from a swing set ending in a dull thud and moans from two girls holding their stomachs in disbelief. We now realized, wait, we can't bungee jump with chains that don't bounce. We then in retrospect saw how utterly absurd the entire venture was! Now as an adult, I still sometimes revert back to that little girl, bungee jumping in a chain swing. I make a decision or choose a road when I didn't truly consider the end result. It's called "reaping and sowing." This goes for bungee jumping in swings and bad choices in life. Whatever choice you make, job you try and road you travel, these will have an end result. I am learning more and more on my journey, consider the end result. Pray and ask God to reveal how this choice might end or what direction it may take your life. Ask, " is this God's will?" Life lesson? Don't bungee jump from a chain swing and find yourself moaning in regret when you hit the bottom.

A true friend is a like a book. You read, you live and then for a time you must close. But, when you return you open right to the very page you left off and resume. Ready to live the next adventure together, anticipating what the next chapter holds, but always remembering the pages gone before.

The same rain that makes the trees to grow in the spring, is the very rain that shakes the leaves from their secure fortresses among the branches and ushers them into a new season each fall. I think God must be very much like the rain. Growing us, nurturing us, but in due season shaking us from our comfortable positions and secure dwellings and taking us into the next season of life. When the autumn rains come and pelt your life, be ready my friends and fall into the arms of your Loving Father.

*apostrophe to the wind*

Sweep ore! The Plains and mountains vast
Sweep on Oh wind! With your deathly blast
Sweep on and ore! The barren hill
Sweep with your gust, your mighty shrill
Across the lilting timbers wide
Across the crystal rivulet you stride
Within the shadiest mountain cove
Within each blossoming valley grove
Beyond the slumbering ocean deep
Beyond the purple horizon you creep
Between the rising summits high
Between the clouds scuttling in the sky
Beside the meadows of grasses deep

Beside the golden fields of wheat
About me yet I feel you beat
A gentle whisper of fragrance sweet
I fain would hear your faintest rasp
Yet quail within at your mighty grasp
Blow on! With sublime and misty gusts
Sweep across the terrestrial, languid dust
Providence alone hath doffed the dam
The reservoir between you and man
By His own bid your bands are freed
His will doth wreak your gust and speed
Sweep on Oh Wind! Relinquish nor refrain
Your breaths to post upon man's fragile frame-

Poem penned as part of a senior high-school assignment. I loved every minute of that project!

You have two windows by which the world can peer into your very heart and soul. Every time you look someone in the eyes, they read a little more about you. Ask yourself, "what story am I telling?"

You are a chrysalis of boundless possibilities. Much of what you may be or the beauty you hold within you is still unseen by the world. The vibrancy, the vitality, the flutter of your wings as He blows His divine breath under you and gives you flight. By His good hand, you are emerging into something extraordinary. Never forget this friends.

# journey on with a purposefully beautiful life

BEAUTIFUL AND SPECIAL MOMENTS CAN be created. Sometimes they just happen, but often we can deliberately design memories, traditions and adventures that make life more beautiful and something that will live forever in our hearts. I have been very blessed to grow up in a family environment that fosters traditions and rich times together. Purposeful steps have been taken to make memories we will never forget. Every Thanksgiving, my Nonny and Pappy come to our home for the evening meal. While the turkey is roasting to a golden perfection, the casseroles are bubbling in the oven and the hot buttery rolls are browning, we began a tradition. Now, granted, we are country folk and live on a farm where we can make this happen, but we all go outside and target practice with our firearms while we wait! In a blaze of noise and smoke we compete for the sharpest shooter or just have fun trying all the different guns my Pappy will bring along. He always brings more ammo than he can use, just so we have enough and always brings his most unique guns to let us try. Daddy and Matt will bring out their firearms and we all get a turn! It has nurtured wonderful family ties and memories! Every Thanksgiving we also make homemade, from scratch pies with my Nonny. She has done this for nearly as long as I can remember. One year she even let every single person select their own " favorite" and together we made probably 14 pies!!! Pretty incredible deliberate decision on her part to make a special moment! It has been so sweet to bake alongside her, learn from her and now she has given us her pie recipes. This is a beautiful time I cherish that will be carried on forever. Each Christmas and birthday morning, Mama has baked a homemade coffee cake. This is something we all look forward to and this recipe will always be special. Christmas Eve we cook a traditional meal of broccoli cheese soup, cheddar biscuits, side salad and carbonated grape juice. We have all grown to anticipate this time around the Christmas table with lights glistening and candles and hearts glowing. We even own special dishes for this time of the year! Setting the table and using holiday place settings has created a wonderful memory, even the process of picking them out and collecting each piece over the years has made it all the richer. My MawMaw and PawPaw's house holds traditions too. A Christmas will not pass that MawMaw has not made her famous Forgotten Cookies and a pan of decadent fudge. They turn out to perfection every year and all the children and grandchildren have come to anticipate this tradition, whether they realize it or not. It doesn't have to be recipes,

feasts and food. It could be the sacrifices you make for someone that they will never forget. Like all the times my Nonny, Pappy, MawMaw and Pawpaw would drive all over the country to support us when we were competing in music or performing at a special venue. I will never forget how special I felt and how unforgettable that made my journey. Or the times my Mama and Daddy went out of their way to let me know they love me. It can be so simple. For instance, when all three of us girls were probably 14 and under and Matt was a baby, they hooked up our little green trailer full of hay bales to the vehicle, ordered pizza and surprised us with a hay ride down our dirt road, eating pizza and singing Christmas songs. Complicated? No. But, I will never forget it as long as I live. It was wonderful. The times Daddy helped us build our tree fort or we sat on the swing set covered in a tent made of bed sheets in the rain, eating grapes we picked off our vine in the front yard. Or Mom taking us on drives down country backroads, flea marketing or getting a frozen coke at our favorite spot or reading stories in the evening all cozied up at her feet. Impromptu trips, drives and meals that made life purposefully beautiful, deliberately special and immensely meaningful. It doesn't cost a lot, but it does require a heart willing to invest in others and a mind that says, "I will purposefully make this a beautiful journey for everyone around me and do all in my power to make it one they won't soon forget."

One is never too old to be corrected. One is never too wise to possibly be in the wrong.

Don't ever think you won't amount to much. I have found some of the tiniest, most insignificant looking seeds to grow into some of the most beautiful and unique plants. Let God plant you, He takes care of what grows.

# *journey on whatever the obstacles*

GOD TAKES GREAT DELIGHT IN taking unlikely people and making them something great like the world has never seen. Moses was convinced he wasn't a good speaker. Ruth was just a nobody from Moab. David stooped to moral failure. Esther was an obscure Jewish girl. Noah had no previous experience in ark construction. Rahab was a harlot. Paul zealously persecuted Christians.

Yet, these stories all end so differently. Moses led Israel out of Egypt. Ruth was in the lineage of Jesus. David goes down in history as a "Man After God's Own Heart". Esther becomes Queen and saves her people. Noah builds the ark and is saved. Rahab is forgiven and makes it to Hebrews 11. Paul is a hero of the faith we all remember for " fighting the good fight, finishing His course and keeping the faith."

Friend, maybe you think you are no one, no talent, no prominence, no eloquence, no one that God would ever think to use.

Please remember, He takes the nobody and makes them someone in Him. He takes the gifts He gave you and says go and I will work in your weakness. He takes your tongue and says I will speak through you. He takes pleasure in taking what the world expects the least from and raising them up as a mighty tool in the Almighty's Hand!

The key is letting Him have His way. We often run when He comes our direction. Sadly many never find out what He could have done with their life, if completely surrendered. Surrender today and watch God move!

Be sure and not look in your rearview mirror of life too much, unless it is to look back and smile, seeing how far God has brought you.

Ask questions, seek advice, learn from those whose boots have worn down the path you are traveling and whose maps bear tear stains and sweat drops.

# *journey on knowing you are not alone*

## Ravens Still Fly

Waiting by a brook in the middle of nowhere
It seemed the world against him, did anyone even care?
Waiting on the Lord, in the desert he would stay
He was not forsaken, but cared for everyday
Elijah was at Cherith, my friend where are you?
A place alone and quite, are you even getting through?
Elijah must have wondered very much the same
God answered with assurance as the Ravens surely came

Are you deep in despair?
Feel like nobody cares
You can't find your way
Or the words to even pray
Just hold on He's not gone
Rest by the brook
Take another look
Lift your eyes to the sky
Ravens still fly

Elijah did not know if he would starve and surely die
But God sent the Ravens with food from on high
Answers, they took wings and came down from Heaven

Blessings from the Lord came down with the Ravens
Miracles still happen when it seems like nothing can
Despite your situation God still has a plan
He cannot forget you in your desert of life
Cast your eyes toward the Heaven
And see Ravens still fly

Do you feel you've been forgotten?
Has life taken its toll?
The God that sent the Ravens
Is still in control

Are you deep in despair?
Feel like nobody cares
You can't find your way
Or the words to even pray
Just hold on, He's not gone
Rest by the brook, take another look
Lift your eyes to the sky
Ravens still fly-
(Song written by my siblings and me)

# journey on no matter what

IT WAS A STEAMY SUMMER day and I was in my usual habitat, tending my garden. I was admiring a bed of flourishing zinnias. Those truly must be the precious gemstones of God's garden, I find them to be one of the loveliest blooms of all. The butterflies must think so too. Because every year when these blossoming beauties burst forth in colorful array it seems the local nature telegraph goes out to all local butterflies and in no time, they arrive. They spend their summer flitting from bloom to bloom sipping nectar like we do sweet tea and lemonade in the south. What a way to spend those hot, sultry days! On this particular afternoon, I was watching two butterflies. The first one I noticed appeared battered. If butterflies have battles to fight, this one would be the battle scarred warrior. It had apparently endured a lot or been through something intense, indeed, the front lines of conflict. It's right wing was missing an entire piece from the backside, it's color was dull and faded and yet, there it was steadily doing what butterflies do. The second butterfly floated over on a winsome breeze and landed nearby. It's appearance was flawless, as if it had just emerged from it's chrysalis. The wings were velvety and glossy. The color was intense and vibrant. It seemed youthful, if there is such a look to be seen in butterflies. I stood there in silence gazing at both. One tattered and worn, the other vivacious and beautiful. Yet, they were both butterflies, both doing what butterflies do. The worn wings and missing back piece didn't deter the one from getting out and collecting nectar and moving from zinnia to zinnia. I thought, this is us. Some of us have been through a lot. Whether it's the wear and tear from mere years of life or the battle wounds you bear and scars from hurt you have been forced to endure. Or maybe a piece of your heart is missing and it gives you a rougher exterior. Perhaps you are full of life, struggles have been few, battles scarce and your determination and optimistic outlook have not been daunted by repeated wounds or the haunting reminder of that missing piece of wing. Whoever you are in the Christian life, you are still a butterfly. You must carry on, you must get up, go out and collect that nectar, move from flower to flower, do what you were made to do, regardless of what you have been through or not been through. God gives the grace to go on in spite of these things that weaken us. God made you to be a an integral part of His Kingdom. You must keep on, keeping on for His glory and Great Name. Day in and day out, just keep doing what you were made to do, faithfully and diligently. By the way, I never saw the tattered butterfly side glance at the beautiful one and hang it's head in shame, nor the flawless ones turn it's little nectar sipping nose to the air in disdain. We are all at different places in our lives and journeys. Be loving, be kind, be faithful and be what God made you to be.

Life holds a lot of fool's gold. We get so caught up in hoarding it away, we let the real gold nuggets slip right through our greedy hands. Don't settle for the sparkle alone, make sure it's genuine.

Never grow too old to play hide and seek. Never grow too sophisticated for funny faces. Never grow too picky that leftovers won't do. Never grow too good for front porches and rocking chairs. Never grow too important for those who believed in you when you were nothing. Never grow too busy for checkers and sweet tea. Never grow too big for make believe battles and horses made of sticks. Never grow too mature to hug mama in front of anybody and everybody. Never grow far from God's Word. Never grow to believe you are any kind of self made special creation, for when you do, you are indeed losing what others have grown to love.

# journey on with a prepared life

I HAVE GROWN UP WITH A passionate love for gardening. I mean, plunging my hands into a bed of soft earth and pulling out a giant wriggling worm is just pretty wonderful! Planting a seed, watering and watching it push itself through the tender earth and begin a glorious transformation has always been grand to me. Everyone wants to see the pretty garden. I mean, what's not to love about an entryway laden heavy with scarlet runner beans and morning glory blossoms of azure? Or the zinnias in almost more colors than I knew existed in the rainbow? Or the sunflowers towering above everything else, just beaming down grinning from ear to ear!? These are all the bountiful pleasures that everyone enjoys, but I've discovered less than excited reactions to wheelbarrow loads of manure, shovels of chicken litter and compost by the buckets. You see, we all relish results, but what it takes to get the results? Not so much. I would completely assure you, that if my garden was left to bloom and next season I went out planted my seed without amending my soil and just expected the process to repeat, I would be sorely disappointed. It takes the hours of preparation, toil and unpleasant work to reap the fragrant blossoms and delicious veggies later in the season. Your life is no different. Don't get so caught up in just wanting the pretty, picture perfect exterior for all the onlookers, that you neglect constantly feeding your character and soul. This takes weeding out what shouldn't be there, feeding and nurturing the good and replenishing the nutrients that get "spent." Let your life be a bountiful garden, brimming full of testimonies to God's goodness and beauty and watch what He grows!

---

Some people are bent on blocking the light. They smother all around them in an enormous, dismal cloud. God made you to live in light and be light. Redirect and reach for The Son.

---

I rise to find the eastern sun drenching the dewy sod
I look upon the waking world to see the stirring of God
His breath catches my carefree hair His might my finite heart
I know He smiles upon me when I feel the shadows part
For every little raindrop and all the flowers in field
Each cricket and meadowlark that with their songs will still
Tell of their glorious Maker, our loving God above
Who every morning bends down Himself to kiss the world with love.
- Poem penned 2017

# journey on knowing from whence your help comes

PSALMS 121:1&2-" I WILL LIFT up mine eyes unto the hills, from whence cometh my help. My help cometh from the LORD, which made heaven and earth."

One of the absolute easiest ways to trip yourself up on your journey is to begin to believe all the good things people say about you. The compliments on your talents, looks, abilities and accomplishments, if not kept in check, will begin to sound sweet and you agree with that grand resume! Before long it takes over your spirit and an arrogance slips out, without you even recognizing it anymore. It's who you are. The people that know you best see it, but you fail to even take a second glance at what you have allowed to grow. One of the biggest things I must constantly deal with, is never starting to believe the nice things people tell me at the product table after a concert. I can allow them to encourage me, and they do. I can allow them to help me, and they do. I can allow God to use them to send some sunshine when I need it, and they do. But, I must never walk away and begin to believe, "yeah, I really am something great." Let me share a very personal way that I believe God reminds me of this very regularly. When I am on stage during a concert, there is a lot, a whole lot going through my mind. Sometimes out of no where I will completely mind blank on where my fingers go next or what chord comes next. I've played it a million times, but suddenly I

am blank. It is in these moments I sometimes send up a flare prayer for help and I feel God bending down and whispering, " You need me Lindsay. That is what you would be without me on your own. That is you. This is Me helping you. I am your help and strength." I believe it with all my heart. I know me. I know how I blank and forget and how weak I am alone. God's Good Hand sustains me and enables me. Why don't you stop right now and thank Him for being that help in your life and if you have started believing the lie that it's all you...... why don't you ask Him to forgive you today?

# journey on with a road map

IT WAS A BEAUTIFUL SUMMER evening on our front porch and we were relishing the last golden glimmers of light from the setting sun, when a small green visitor made its way across the floor. My sister bent down to pick up what was a tiny green inchworm. We all watched as he began moving again and making "inches" as quickly as possible. She looked at the little guy that seemed so determined to get moving and said "I wonder if He knows where He is going and will He know when he gets there?" What a question! I couldn't help but put that question to myself and now I ask it to you? "Do you know where you are going and will you know when you get there?" Proverbs 4:26-"Ponder the path of thy feet, and let all thy ways be established." What goals do you have? Are you on a specific course charted out by wise counsel and Scripture? Are you heading somewhere? Anywhere in particular? Are you following a map of deliberate purpose or are you wandering in circles until someone points you in a general direction? I have had trouble in the past answering the classic question-"where do you see yourself in 10 years?" I often found myself groping for an intelligent sounding answer while still questioning if it was accurate. I finally realized, you may not know the details 10 years down the road, but if you have a charted course you have a general idea of where you are going to wind up. Proverbs 3:5-6" Trust in the LORD with all thine heart; and lean not unto thine own understanding. In all thy ways acknowledge him, and he shall direct thy paths." I couldn't think of a better place to turn when making a map of life than the All Seeing, All Knowing Map Maker that sees the end before I ever come near reaching it. The absolute ultimate question is "do you know your eternal destination?" Are you Blood washed and bound for Heaven? Oh! and the beauty is, we will know when we have reached our destination, for we will know our Savior's face! So, the challenge today? "Do you know where you are going and will you know when you get there?" As for you and me let's make a map and say yes! As for the inchworm? Well, I don't think we'll ever know.

Isaiah 26:3-4 Thou wilt keep him in perfect peace, whose mind is stayed on thee: because he trusteth in thee. Trust ye in the LORD for ever: for in the LORD JEHOVAH is everlasting strength:

Psalms 37:3-7 Trust in the LORD, and do good; so shalt thou dwell in the land, and verily thou shalt be fed. Delight thyself also in the LORD: and he shall give thee the desires of thine heart. Commit thy way unto the LORD; trust also in him; and he shall bring it to pass. And he shall bring forth thy righteousness as the light, and thy judgment as the noonday. Rest in the LORD, and wait patiently for him: fret not thyself because of him who prospereth in his way, because of the man who bringeth wicked devices to pass.

Jeremiah 29:11-13 For I know the thoughts that I think toward you, saith the LORD, thoughts of peace, and not of evil, to give you an expected end. Then shall ye call upon me, and ye shall go and pray unto me, and I will hearken unto you. And ye shall seek me, and find me, when ye shall search for me with all your heart.

# journey on above and beyond

IT WAS THE PERFECT SUNDAY afternoon. I was sitting in a tiny rural town in middle Tennessee known as "Bell Buckle." Even the name stirs images of the quintessential small town USA. Big front porches, sweet tea and moon pies. And you would be 100% correct. A part of this town never moved on with modern society. It has retained all the most beautiful elements of the "good ole days," while giving people today the glimmer of hope that this way of life is still alive and well. I found myself perched on an idyllic ice cream parlor porch with the strains of old retro songs infiltrating the summer air. I was enjoying my peach yogurt milkshake immensely when a shiny black truck pulled up to the curb near me. I looked their way and our eyes met, we smiled. All southern folk look each other in the eyes and smile. This older couple appeared to be looking for something. She leaned toward me and my milkshake and asked, " do you know how much an ice cream cone is? We can't walk well, it's hard to get out

of the truck." I said, " I don't, but I can find out!" I opened the shop door, the little overhead bell rang announcing my re-entry and the owner came to the counter. I explained there was an older couple who couldn't walk well and they were interested in knowing the price for cones. I had hardly finished my sentence or the imaginary period was barely in place when he, without hesitation said, "Oh, I'll just go out to them!" That he did. The owner spent quite some time at their truck door, curbside. He went back into the shop and reappeared with two strawberry pink ice cream cones. Hand dipped and hand delivered to their truck. Goodbyes exchanged, he went back inside to continue his business. I looked around. His shop was crowded, his customers happily licking cones and two very pleased senior citizens were driving away that had been treated with kindness and respect. It was no wonder. The work ethic and business model for this shop was clearly a step above the care and thoughtfulness much of the rest of the world sees. I smiled. This should be all of us. This should at the very least be every soul that claims the name "Christian." We should be going the extra mile, making the effort and treating those around us with love, respect and unusually kind care. Believe me, it will command the attention of the world. It will turn some heads and it will change some lives. Why don't we strive to go the extra mile today, my friend?

John 13:34-35 A new commandment I give unto you, That ye love one another; as I have loved you, that ye also love one another. By this shall all men know that ye are my disciples, if ye have love one to another.

# *journey on making right your wrong*

I WAS ABOUT 11 AND MY sister about 9. There were few places any more fascinating in our minds than our PawPaw's cabinet mill. We were allowed to ride around on dollies, play with air hoses, make random small wooden creations and sit in his office and feel big. This particular visit we were sitting in the office going through his drawers when we came across a bottle of white out. Now granted, I take full responsibility for the following events, but my sister sure didn't put up any protest! For some unknown reason that I can't even figure out to this very day, I suggested we take the white out and paint our nails. Now, I suggested this completely believing that a quick trip to the cabinet mill water fountain would remove all evidence of our deed. I truly believed that no one would ever know. As an adult now, I know how every story ends where the kid banked on that theory. Not so good! We painted each nail tediously and with delight admired our masterpiece. I must have tried to rub it off and realized it wasn't moving or peeling or anything. I panicked and dashed out of the office for the water fountain. My sister followed closely behind. I had her press the fountain on and I began frantically rubbing my white out nails under cold water of all things. Nothing was happening. She tried, I tried, we kept trying until most of it was gone. It's a wonder we had nails left on our hands. There was only small specks of white and we figured that would be easy enough to conceal. We got back to our grandparent's home that night and were snuggled up in our makeshift pallets on the floor, sandwiched between layers of grandma's blankets. We thought we had made it. We were in bed, Mom hadn't said anything, we supposed she hadn't noticed our hands. We were just getting ready to doze off and mom walked in the room. She was holding my dress. She said, " I was washing your clothes and found white out on your dress, why would that be?" My guilty little heart sank. Yes, and as they say confession is good for the soul! We confessed, but what gets me to this day is why we ever did it to start with. We knew we weren't to mess with white out, moreover paint nails with it. We then knew not to hide it, but we did. We knew better than to do any of it. I'm pretty sure this is a lot of us today. We know better than to say those words, treat that individual that way, represent Christ in that light or walk down that road. Yet, we sometimes do it and unfortunately sometimes think we can just bury it in the back corner and no one will notice. It will find you, it will surface. If you have hurt someone, make it right. If you have badly represented Christ, repent and make Him look good starting now. If you have walked down a road you should have never gone, you can by God's grace turn around. I'm so thankful for second chances. Let's turn over a new leaf today.

# journey on all the way to the top

## -The Perfect Day-

THE SKY WAS A PERFECT shade of azure speckled with lazy clouds that were in no hurry to go anywhere. Kinda like the turtles we had back home that crossed the roads as if they were the only traffic, slow and easy. Sunbeams were kissing my face and dappling the world around me. Looked like God had dropped a bag of gold dust on everything, it just shimmered! All creation seemed alive and beat with a pulse of vibrancy that was ready to conquer, to achieve, to accomplish the uncommon. I had long waited for this day. Actually, you might could say I dreamed about it 364 days previously. Now it was here. We strapped on our backpacks and filled them with snacks and water. Although, as I will note later, not nearly enough water. I felt equipped and ready, except for one item of contention. Apparently none of us had appropriate shoes for such a trek as was ahead of us. The concern rattled around in the back of our preoccupied minds and then got lost somewhere between the adrenaline rush and excitement of the moment. So off we went. I'm not sure who you are reading this, but if you're like me, an exploration outdoors brings out the most adventurous side of my being. I mean, I suddenly feel like Lewis and Clark heading across unmapped territory, upstream for the unknown, or pioneers bound westward on the Oregon Trail, or Daniel Boone walking the "Dark and Bloody Ground." All my fancy dreaming and notions aside, it was sure to be an adventure. I wasn't going to find the Pacific Ocean, or blaze the trail for others to settle one day, or even bring people to live in the dangerous territory of Kentucky, but little did I know, I was going to discover something even greater. Yes, I was finally in Yosemite National Park and it was a perfect day.

## -Daunting Statistics-

The goal on this fine day in May was ascending the granite mountain to the very top of Yosemite Falls. Let me give you a few statistics before we begin the journey. The entire hike would be 7.2 miles round trip. You came down, exactly the same way you went up. We would ascend 2,700 feet and encounter dozens of hairpin switchbacks. The entire

hike would take 6-8 hours round-trip and it was classified "Strenuous." Let me make a little "Lindsay Note" right here. When you see the word "strenuous" on a hike analysis, just immediately translate to the following definition.

Strenuous: A level of extreme and unmatched difficulty resulting in exhaustion, fatigue and the inability to put one foot in front of the other, often accompanied by heaving and gasping for breath.

You will thank me for that definition when you get ready for your next strenuous hike! To be honest, we read all the statistics before setting out on the hike. 7.2 miles, 2,700 feet, dozens of switchbacks, strenuous, okay, no problem! It seemed so achievable from the base of the mountain with full water bottles, plenty of snacks, feet that at least weren't hurting yet and tons of energy. The real test was not how enthused we were at the trail's entrance, but were we going to make it all the way? Were we going all the way to the top?

## -So It Begins-

My spirits were high! I was breathing in the fresh, mountain air and exhilarated in body and spirit about the entire day ahead of me. We entered the trailhead and so it began. The early path was a fairly good trail, mostly dirt and some rocks to watch your footing on. But, as you can imagine it instantly started moving up. There was obvious incline from the onset. Of course I shocked myself when not very far into it at all, I decided that those giant granite boulders on the sides of the trail were for people like me and I collapsed on one and proceeded to catch my breath. I figured this was not a race, but an endurance course, boy was I right. This pattern continued even early on, walk, stop, drink, try and breath. We encountered all types of people on the trail. Multiple languages, countries, old and young. One particular young Frenchman had me staring in disbelief. He apparently had a lot to say and was talking without hardly breathing and at the same time passing us. I was in awe, I could barely breath, let alone start talking a hundred miles an hour! They disappeared around the bend, still telling his story. We did begin to recognize certain groups of people. They would pass you, then you would pass them resting and this pattern of catch up and pass on happened the entire journey up the mountain. I just didn't realize yet how few I would recognize at the top.

## -Columbia Rock-

As the trek ensued the difficulty obviously did also, but the views began to exceed our expectations. The grandeur of this hike was hitting me and I kept staring out to my right, just soaking in the supreme majesty. It was about this time people were passing us, but going in the opposite direction. They were going down the mountain. We inquired, "how far to the top, did you go all the ways?" The answer was no, they had only gone as far as Columbia Rock. Wow, I thought, go to Columbia Rock but not all the ways. I had no great gauge of how far we had even come or how far we had to go, except for the fact that my body was telling me I had hiked a million miles already. We pressed on. Finally, up ahead we could see a gathering of people and an apparent overlook of a great rock that hung over the Yosemite Valley. We had arrived at Columbia Rock and I must say, the view was spellbinding. People were sprawled out on boulders trying to regain composure and oxygen intake, while others posed for photos with the insanely gorgeous view behind them, documenting that they had indeed arrived at Columbia Rock. I was so pleased, but it wasn't where we were stopping. We had set out for the top and as beautiful as this was, I knew something better lay ahead. But, usually the best things in life come with a bigger price tag and this one was significantly more than Columbia Rock.

## When It Sounds Like Thunder

It was getting rough. Columbia Rock and on began the real challenge. My legs and feet began to feel as if someone had taken them, filled them with lead marbles and said "now, keep hiking!" They felt so heavy! One foot trying to go in front of the next seemed like a monumental achievement every time it happened! The trail began to get very rough, lots of rocks cropping out of the dirt and your footing had to be watched ever so closely. The incline grew ever steeper. Suddenly our ears tuned into a low roar. As we kept walking the roar began to sound like something was wrong. It mimicked that of thunder rumbling aggressively or perhaps what I would imagine an avalanche to sound like. A soft mist began to fall on us and we probably looked like children in their first snowfall. The excitement of such cool refreshment sprinkling our weary beings was evident. We had been using the cool streams all along the way to douse our faces, necks and heads. Each stream seemed a little oasis on this great mountain and brought our body temperatures down each time we splashed the Icy water upon us. Then we rounded the bend in the trail and it appeared. It was Yosemite Falls roaring like a lion in its might and dangerous strength. It's colossal size and volume of water being forced over the fall's precipice made for the cloud of mist that just silently hung over this section of the trail. We felt encouraged. Although we could see we were not near the top of this phenomenon, we were getting ever so much closer. As we hiked on, the eerie roar of this natural beast hounded us for quite some time. I realized, when it sounds like thunder, prepare for rain.

## 30 Minutes

Now my legs felt lead filled and iron shackled! I was considering just getting on my hands and knees and commencing to crawling the rest of the ways. The incline took drastic measures to prove to us we were surely getting closer. It was common practice on the trail to ask updates or distance left from fellow travelers on the hike. We met a mother/Daughter team coming down. I completely assumed that meeting them so very far into this journey, they must have summited the mountain. We asked if they had and to my shock they said, no. She said we made it a ways from here but it gets really rough. Then she commented that coming down was hard on the knees. Oh boy, that was a thought. I was busy thinking about surviving in one piece going up, but as they say, "what goes up must come down!" I was commencing to feel like Pilgrim in "Pilgrim's Progress" with the travelers going the opposite direction crying "turn back!" Although nothing quite as dramatic as this took place, I did turn to my sister Sarah and tell her how I felt. Yet, we were going. There was no way we could stop now. We began asking travelers "how far to the top?" The consistent answer was "Oh, about 30 minutes." 2 hours later we were completely convinced that your estimating skills must be affected by the extreme altitude. We were still hiking and it was the longest 30 minutes of our lives! Somewhere around this point, we met a bright eyed Oriental lady in a wide brimmed sun hat and an incredible excess of energy, that I wished I had! She came up behind us on the trail. We struck up a conversation about her trip to America and she was beaming with excitement and gratefulness at her opportunity to see such beauty and experience it! A comment was made about the top and I said something about the "good things not coming easy"." She concurred with an invigorating comment about "great things in life you have to work for." We had to stop and catch our breath, she passed us and as she did, she said "see you at the top." And I believed her, I had no doubt I would see her again.

## We Were There

I know people say the final stretch of a race can be the hardest. I would completely agree with that analysis. We had hiked for hours, our bodies were growing weary and not to mention the water rations had been dismally diminished. We were now conserving water in order to have some when we summited and for the hike down. We passed a trio hiking up and one young lady in the group was apparently struggling. It was not easy for her, but she had come so far. I was very impressed with her determination and tenacity. Another young man from Asia, probably around India, was hiking alone. Come to find out his friend was going at a much faster pace and he told him to go on ahead and he would catch up. We got acquainted on one of our stops to regain our strength and try to take in that commodity that felt so very lacking-oxygen! He kinda followed behind us for a ways, then at some point he disappeared. We knew we had to be in the final stages. People were growing sparser than before.

We encountered one man who was waiting for his friend. He had been at the top and was heading down. That seemed encouraging, he had been there and from his description and his friend's, we weren't too far. We felt their estimation was more accurate since they had just come down. We kept on. Our faces were flushed, our legs barely operating and our breaths short and heavy. I kept thinking, surely we are close. Then we encountered a couple who must have seen the extreme and vulnerably honest look of exhaustion on our faces and said with a smile,"y'all are almost there. It's just like 15 minutes, we know, we were just there." Now that's someone to bank your hopes on! They were just there and we were 15 minutes away! I had confidence that it wouldn't be hours, but mere minutes and I would actually conquer this mountain that was desperately trying to conquer me with a vengeance.

I kept thinking, they were there,15 minutes!

## All The Way To The Top

15 minutes passed slowly but surely. I knew we had reached the summit when I saw signs for other alternate hiking paths for those bound toward more distant destinations. But, I still couldn't see the view or the falls plummeting over to the valley floor below. We kept walking, but with a grand new vigor, because it was fairly flat on top, we just had to get to the edge now! I don't have words to adequately express what my heart and eyes took in on the summit of that mountain. I felt like a bird, free on the wind, sailing above everything. Literally on top of the world. The valley floor appeared small and almost play like. Like tiny pieces from a movie set. The world I was in was large and vast, touching the sky with my fingertips, hemmed about by giant boulders and trees and the thunderous roar of that magnificent phenomenon crashing over the precipice. It was surreal. We made it! After a few pictures, we all collapsed on the massive granite boulders and just lay there, relishing the fact that we had indeed summited. We pulled out some snacks and a little rationed water. I looked over and there was that trio, with the young lady who had indeed made it to the top! I was so happy for her. Then from behind me appears a bright eyed lady in a wide brimmed sunhat. I knew she would be there. I never doubted it for a second. She was equally enthused, taking in every moment and all the grandeur. I felt so aware of God's strength, might and majesty. I now realize what I felt like looking at the little valley below like it was a play set for a child. Then I think of the verse in Psalms 8:4-"What is man, that thou art mindful of him? and the son of man, that thou visitest him?"

How absolutely insignificant we must look to the Almighty God peering through the portals of Heaven onto little specks of creation down below. I don't know, but I really didn't pay a lot of attention to one specific car driving through the valley as I peered down. It was all insignificant to me. But God, I'm so glad He's different. It really puts life into perspective and makes me say "thank you God, for noticing me, loving me and listening to me."

Well, after photos, a video, resting, snacks and walking over to see the river that fed the famous Yosemite Falls, we decided we should probably head down. Like I said earlier, you go down the exact trail you came up.

No zip line or curly slide shortcuts! Although, I'll drop that in the Yosemite Suggestion box! As we were getting ready to go, here he comes. Our Asian friend had finally made it! It took him much longer, but he kept on and he did it! All the faces at the top wore a similar look of achievement, fulfilment and supreme happiness, oh and just a tinge of exhaustion that was beginning to melt into a memory. I recognized faces, but so few faces were actually accounted for. Where was everyone? The trail had lots of people, but the the top held the few, the few that knew from the beginning, they were going all the way to the top.

## Lessons I Learned From The Top

During and after the hike that day, I remember things that struck me profoundly and left impressions on my mind and heart. I want to parallel these with the trek and share them with each of you.

In life there will be key decisions thrown at you. It is in these moments you must decide what path to choose or how far you want to go. Some people in life are content with a good, productive and even an extremely successful life, but they don't really care to go all the way. I would call this the "Columbia Rock" of our world. Seems like it could almost be an absolute destination in itself. It was hard to achieve, never easy, the benefits once you got there were incredible. So, one can see how simple it would be to become very content only ever arriving at "Columbia Rock." After all, most people are still at the base of the mountain just staring at the trailhead, we actually made it to Columbia Rock, what's so bad with that? Herein is the question we must each answer individually. How far do you want to go? Above Columbia Rock is a lot more climbing, difficulties, challenges and people that will tell you to turn back while the getting is good. But, you know deep in your heart there is something better, something bigger, something that if you are willing to sweat and toil you can achieve for your own. The real temptation is not the base of the mountain, or the inclination to just pull up an easy chair and make camp at the trail head. The deceptive temptation is the people who set out and achieve, but stop at what is in all reality a counterfeit for the real deal. Columbia Rock was a grand place, but there was something grander. Being able to discern the difference is key. You will often be able to identify achievers. No, they aren't the flawless ones, that never mess up, never seem to be caught out of breath by life or never travel slow. They are the steady, the consistent, the determined. They sweat, they fall, they collapse, they crawl, but they are always moving. They see life as a challenge and they embrace it with both arms, all their heart and an open mind. They ask questions, they seek advice, they evaluate why they fell and what they can do to change their shortcomings. Achievers bear an unmatched sparkle in their eye that defies the naysayers and voices that call out, "turn back, you'll never make it!" The unquenchable thirst within them will never be appeased by "almosts" and "nearly as goods." They set out to go all the way to the top and to the top they will go. Throw perfection out the window and let insecurity sink in the river. You will fall. You will have to sweat and crawl and eat dirt to get to the top, but you can and you will. Determine that by the Grace of God you want His best and you want to do your best to live this life to the fullest. Life is a gift unmatched by anything else and we should live it like the treasure it is. Going all the way to the top in life is ensuring just that. Let me leave you with this final thought my friends,-

When the odds say you can't. When the world says you shouldn't. When the skeptics say it's risky. When your heart beats in fear. Remember, God says you can, you will, you'll succeed and fear not. For any door He opens He will take you through and any dream He embeds within your soul, He will bring it to pass. So….Dream On.

See You At The Top.

## Before Your Journey To The Top

Before heading for the top my friend, I would like to share with you the one and only way you will ever make it truly successfully, with true happiness and eternal fulfillment. That is with Jesus Christ living within you as your Lord and Saviour. Just as there are few that will make it to the top of life and achievement, the Bible tells us of another group that will be fewer in number.

Matthew 7:14-"Because strait is the gate, and narrow is the way, which leadeth unto life, and few there be that find it."

There has been a way made for you to live eternally in Heaven and escape the penalty of death that was sentenced upon you the moment you were born into sin. Let's first establish that we are all sinners. Have you told one lie, stolen anything, coveted or dishonored someone, however tiny it seems to you, that makes you a sinner. Have you broken just one of the Ten Commandments?

Exodus 20-

1. Thou shalt have no other gods before me
2. Thou shalt not make unto thee any graven image
3. Thou shalt not take the name of the Lord thy God in vain
4. Remember the sabbath day, to keep it holy
5. Honor thy father and thy mother
6. Thou shalt not kill
7. Thou shalt not commit adultery
8. Thou shalt not steal
9. Thou shalt not bear false witness
10. Thou shalt not covet

Would you agree right now that you are a sinner?

Romans 3:23-" For all have sinned, and come short of the glory of God;"

We have all come up short of what it takes to enter Heaven and we stand condemned in our sin. But the story does not end there, praise God!

God loves you and He sent His sinless Son to the cross to pay the price in full for all of your sin. Through the perfect Blood shed at Calvary He has made a way for you to live forever with Him.

John 3:16 & 17-" For God so loved the world, that he gave his only begotten Son, that whosoever believeth in him should not perish, but have everlasting life. For God sent not his Son into the world to condemn the world; but that the world through him might be saved."

He wants you to live with Him in Heaven and escape the wrath of hell. But, there is just one way. It is not you, or your good works, or going to church on Easter and Christmas or being nice to the neighbor you can't stand. Whoever you are reading this right now, if I could call you by name I would, please understand this truth. Good works, acts of penance, going to church, a denomination or even baptism will not under any condition save you or secure a home in Heaven.

Ephesians 2:8 & 9 –"For by grace are ye saved through faith; and that not of yourselves: it is the gift of God: Not of works, lest any man should boast."

Titus 3:5 Not by works of righteousness which we have done, but according to his mercy he saved us, by the washing of regeneration, and renewing of the Holy Ghost;"

If getting in Heaven depended on your exemplary behavior or good works, then you could be downright proud of it and boastful and it would also cease being a " free gift" because now you " earned it." But this is simply not the case, you cannot and never will do anything, ever that gets you into Heaven. It is a free gift that we have nothing to do with, except receive it.

Romans 6:23-" For the wages of sin is death; but the GIFT of God is eternal life through Jesus Christ our Lord."

My friend, if good works are what you have been relying on to get you to Heaven, there is good news for you yet- Stop trying to earn your way and fall on God's mercy alone today!

The one and only way is through Jesus Christ, His sinless blood and His finished work at Calvary.

1 John 1:7-" ……..and the blood of Jesus Christ his Son cleanseth us from all sin."

That is the narrow way few people will find. It is so simple, but so many people will reject it and try to create their own way and in the end hear these tragic words-

Matthew 7:23-"And then will I profess unto them, I never knew you: depart from me, ye that work iniquity."

If I could look you in the eyes now, I would plead with you to understand the importance of getting this nailed down. Maybe you haven't tried good works. Maybe you are as lost as lost can be and you know it. Maybe you have been running from God or pretending. Please friend, stop running, drop the façade. Your eternity is too important to waste time on that.

Please hear the voice of Jesus calling to you. He made the way. Actually, He's already gone all the way for you. Will you ask Him to save you today?

1 John 1:9 –" If we confess our sins, he is faithful and just to forgive us our sins, and to cleanse us from all unrighteousness."

Romans 10:9-" That if thou shalt confess with thy mouth the Lord Jesus, and shalt believe in thine heart that God hath raised him from the dead, thou shalt be saved."

"For whosoever shall call upon the name of the Lord shall be saved."- Romans 10:13

I pray you call on Him today.

# journey on straight and true

As you continue on your journey, keep this in mind. In order to stay true to God, His Word and His will, our compass must be pointing true. A compass can be set correctly using Gods Word alone as a guide. Fix your compass directly ahead, don't let the easier paths or more attractive views distract you. Believe me fellow traveler, they will. The world will glisten and gleam when the sun hits it, sin will advertise on road signs and look delightful, the wrong way and all its dainties will hound you every moment of everyday. But press on. Keep your eyes straight ahead, keep walking true to what God has set for your life, immerse yourself in His Word, talk to Him constantly and you will cross the finish line strong.

Proverbs 4:25 - 27 "Let thine eyes look right on, and let thine eyelids look straight before thee. Ponder the path of thy feet, and let all thy ways be established. Turn not to the right hand nor to the left: remove thy foot from evil."

Psalms 143:8-
"Cause me to hear thy
lovingkindness in the morning;
for in thee do I trust: cause
me to know the way wherein
I should walk; for I lift up my
soul unto thee."

## "Journey On"

My heart can sometimes fail me
My feet grow tired and sore
Yet my map says I've not made it
And the Map Maker asks for more
The hills are steep and rocky
Easier ways always abound
Yet this path He has charted
Will yield a sweeter crown
So I trust The One that's gone before
Walked the path that I now tread
And this wayfaring Pilgrim's heart
Melts in peace dispersing dread
For my road may not be your road
Yet I'll travel what He designed
So let's Journey On dear Pilgrim
Looking always up as we climb
Journeying On,
Lindsay

Printed in the United States
By Bookmasters